D1555776

AIRBUS A380

SUPERJUMBO ON WORLD TOUR

DAVID MAXWELL

Zenith Press

ACKNOWLEDGMENTS

AirUtopia: To pursue & compliment aviation with respect to all cultures

The Lord Jesus Christ, who deserves all credit for my good fortune. The sacrifices of my mother and father, Dayton and Marie Maxwell, have been unmatched during my years of building AirUtopia. My fiancé Aoy's endless trips to assist me through some of the least hospitable locations are a great tribute to her unselfishness. My longtime trusted friends Mohamed and Maimah Ndiaye for the many years past and upcoming. And a special thank you to Airbus Industrie, Etihad Airways, Lufthansa, and Airbus Flight Test Engineer Jacky Joye and Airbus security for the great tour of the A380 at Al Ain.

A great book is made with the teamwork of a publishing production team who deserves at least as much credit as myself. The team of MBI/Zenith Press includes Richard Kane (Publisher), Scott Pearson (Editorial), Steve Gansen (Editorial), Brenda Canales (Book Design), and Tom Heffron (Cover Design). Many thanks for the continued publishing excellence of this team.

Last, the passion and camaraderie of the team members supporting me are the reason why I am relentless in pursuing our vision. They include Scott Owen, Ma Shek Ching, Brian Nash, Derek States, Saliya Herath, Nipapan Unsuwanchai, Sutisa Jindanon, Simon Wilson, Bruno Pinheiro, and Bruno Misonne. What a great team!

This book is dedicated to all those pioneers in aviation, often unnoticed, who give their lives daily for a near perfect system; for the readers like you, who keep aviation on the forefront of many discussions; and for the supporting team around me . . . as I am only as good as my surrounding team.

On the cover: The A380 dominates a runway in Abu Dhabi, the capital of the United Arab Emirates.

On the frontispiece: Three A380s nestled together under the hot sun at Airbus' factories, where these early test aircraft were assembled.

On the title pages: The A380 F-WWDD taxis for the first time at London Heathrow Airport with numerous British Airways aircraft in attendance.

On the back cover: Testing extreme weather in Addis Ababa, Ethiopia, and Iqaluit, Canada.

Library of Congress Cataloging-in-Publication Data

Maxwell, David, 1969–
   Airbus A380 : superjumbo on world tour / by David Maxwell.
      p. cm.
   ISBN: 978-0-7603-3279-5 (hardbound w/ jacket)
   1. Airbus A380 (Jet transport) I. Title.

TL686.A43M38 2007
629.133'349—dc22

2007029256

Editor: Scott Pearson
Designer: Brenda C. Canales

Printed in China

CONTENTS

Preface   6

section one
First Flights and Preliminary Tests   12
Toulouse   13
Frankfurt   20
Asia and Australia   24
Colombia   36
Iqaluit   38
London Heathrow   46
Al Ain   54
Addis Ababa   61

section two
Air Shows and VIP Tours   66
Paris Air Show   67
Dubai Air Show   74
Asian Aerospace   84
Berlin Air Show ILA   90

Farnborough Air Show   94
Abu Dhabi—Etihad Airways   102
Bangkok—VIP Visit   110
Behind the Scenes   114

section three
Final Tests and Passenger Flights   118
Seoul, South Korea   119
Tokyo, Japan   120
Guangzhou, China   123
Beijing, China   126
Johannesburg, South Africa   130
Vancouver, Canada   131
Qantas Route Proving   132
Lufthansa Route Proving   136
The People and the Passion   154

Contributors   158
Aviation Data Corporation/AirUtopia DVDs 158

Not even the hottest days stopped me from filming the A380, such as this dramatic display over the waters surrounding Changi Airport, Singapore. My fashionable Australian hat and the breathtaking air display helped me achieve my goal.

6

PREFACE

Sitting with an iced coffee in a 1970s-style café in downtown Bangkok, Thailand, I pondered how to solve a problem. I had been trying to get to Japan to complete filming of Tokyo's airports, but Typhoon Nesat (Dante) was battering Japan and canceling flights. As frustration brewed, I happened across an article about the Airbus A380 making its first public flight at the Paris Air Show. I had been aware of this event, but feared that it would be too hard to budget and too risky. As the typhoon delay lengthened, I began to have second thoughts. The A380 would make history around the world, and I wanted to be a part of it. After some quick advice about the show, I called my fiancé, Aoy, to ask her to join me and then purchased a ticket to Paris at the last minute—afraid to fail but not of failure.

I had only one day to capture the entire show. As I entered during one of the busiest and hottest days in Paris Air Show history, the crowds made it nearly impossible to get the right shots. It was a bad start and I was deeply concerned. There was simply no space. As I stood in near failure, out of nowhere Aoy obtained a special ticket from someone who no longer needed it, and a great location opened up. The crowds were not disappointed as the A380 lifted off and made a steep right turn into the clear blue sky. We had captured this magnificent plane on its first public flight, a miracle considering the elements! Thus the voyage of my team of mostly volunteers began, but failure was possible at every corner of the world tour, and this always kept me on a wing and a prayer.

When I heard at the last minute that the A380 would make its first flight to Frankfurt, Germany, one of the most famous airports in the world, I didn't

superjumbo on world tour

want to miss it. I went uninvited and arrived just in time, but Airbus often does not want a lot of publicity during testing, so finding the right location was difficult. I asked around, followed others, and went through a maze of dead ends, paths, and stairways. It was hit or miss, but after dodging through trees and bushes, I captured the takeoff through a fog at nine o'clock the next morning. The prototype wore a mostly all-white paint scheme, a one-time opportunity; more titles would soon be added. Another sigh of relief for the moment.

As I sat in another country, an article took me by complete surprise: "A380 delayed for Asia/Australia tour due to engine malfunction." The A380 was supposed to have arrived that very day on its first landing in Asia at Singapore for another test flight. Thanks to the report of this malfunction, I had been given forewarning. I immediately studied the flight plan that took the A380 from Toulouse to Singapore and then on to Australia and finally back through Kuala Lumpur for the first arrivals in Asia and Australia. I had time to catch both.

As I sat in the humid heat at Singapore Changi, all landings were occurring on the parallel runway, but I took a chance and stayed on the opposite runway. My gamble was that the A380 would land on the side closer to the Singapore Airlines terminal, but nothing was guaranteed. Finally, as my heart pounded in excitement, the Super Jumbo roared over me fifteen minutes late, and landed exactly where I had anticipated. Up next, the land down under.

Finding the right location in Sydney took a lot of asking around; luckily the Australian people were always welcoming. After long walks with heavy equipment, side-stepping more bushes, and crossing a dangerous highway, the final location depended on the inconsistent winds. I was taking both film and video, but to save money I hadn't brought anyone with me to Sydney. Luckily I was able to quickly teach fellow mate Matt Loewy to take these important photos of Sydney Airport's history. After some practice,

we were ready, and the A380 glided in for a smooth touchdown with Qantas titles. Success and on to Kuala Lumpur.

Three stops later, a tiring journey took me to Kuala Lumpur. Arriving at 4:30 p.m., I joined my long-time friend from Hong Kong, Ma Shek Ching. Thirty minutes later we were outside the terminal and a last-minute thought occurred to me. We ran to the Malaysia Airport Authority, arriving at closing time, but somehow managed to reach Public Relations, and within minutes I was on the phone with the coordinator. Next day we were signed up as part of the press for the A380 ceremony and participated in one of the greatest aviation experiences of my life. The A380 arrived to a special water canon salute with music and dancing. Ministers and other VIPs attended a reception fit for royalty. Then we got our first VIP tour inside the first A380, F-WWOW. The sun was shining, but a massive dark rainstorm was overcoming it from the opposite direction. The lightning and rains hit hard, but not before we pulled away with some heavenly photographs. Now to the coldest place on earth.

I sat in Washington DC preparing for other duties when word came that the A380 was going to land for the first time in North America. Problem was, the location was one of the harshest locations on earth, a desolate icy town called Iqaluit. My great northern colleague, Scott Owen from Canada, briefed me how to get there, and I quickly discovered the shock of the cost of going this far north. After a few stressful hours, I decided that we must take this chance. The entire trip north-ward was stressful; if the oncoming blizzard diverted us to the next nearest airport—nearly two hours away—all expenses would be lost! With a prayer we made a final approach into Iqaluit, and we barely got on the ground before the storm surged in and all visibility was lost.

Iqaluit, with night temperatures of -45°C (-49°F) and a howling wind, was the greatest aviation experience I have had to date!

Nothing compared to being on location and capturing the best angles of the A380 as I traveled the world documenting this amazing aircraft.

The challenges of navigating around the airport, the danger of freezing to death if lost, and the possibility of frozen equipment failures were unforgettable. Throughout this, the Super Jumbo did its overnight cold soak, taxi, and takeoff and landing tests without flaws. We had conquered for just a moment the unforgiving boundaries of the Arctic Circle.

Abu Dhabi, the capital of the United Arab Emirates, was hosting a first-time visit of the A380, including a visit to Middle East airline Etihad and hot weather testing—45°C (113°F)—in El Ain, a desert oasis. With Etihad's cordial assistance, we captured a fantastic flyby past the grand palace and another past Abu Dhabi airport. Finally came touchdown and a tow to a magnificent ceremony dedicating this aircraft to the future of Etihad.

In El Ain, Airbus security allowed us open access to the aircraft before final departure from the desert airport. A private tour was given by Jacky Joye, one of the six Airbus crewmembers to participate in the first A380 flight. This was an unexpected honor and our gratitude goes out to this crew. MSN 4 taxied and lifted off very early with a massive cloud of dust, and I was on my way to the next destination.

The Land of the Rising Sun, denied to me a year and a half earlier, would soon greet us well during A380 global route testing. Arriving in Tokyo, we were given exclusive access to an airport tower in the last hour! We had feared that we would have our first failure, but after walking up to the right person, we were granted access to one of the best overlooks in aviation today, an overview of Narita Airport! It was a cold, rainy day but our hearts were warm as the A380 glided into Narita with helicopters hovering everywhere and thousands of spectators gathered in the vicinity. We were again blessed at the last minute. Would this luck continue?

I had been in China two years before, but the locations I remembered were completely gone because of the construction of a massive new terminal for the Beijing 2008 Olympics. I spent hours moving around the airport, walking through a maze of unorganized paths, tall grass, and remote trails. I stopped, ready to give up, when I ran into another colleague, Lee Bit! Amazingly, Lee told me that there was a gap in the wall giving passage to a very remote public location. Upon arriving there, I was shocked to see that we were nearly alongside the A380 stand—in front of the VIP hall. After climbing more walls and following some brilliant local Chinese spotters, we crawled and climbed our way onto an old house overlooking the ramp. Just an hour earlier this trip seemed lost, and now we had a grandstand location of all activity! Stealth measures had prevailed.

We captured the complete preparations, taxi, and takeoff of the A380 for its voyage to Shanghai from the somewhat inhospitable abandoned rooftop. As I joked about ordering pizza from the United States, my driver, who saw I was ravenous, brought some local lamb sandwiches and coke. My local comrades and I shared food. We were in aviation heaven. A local enthusiast gave me an unforgettable comment: "You are the only foreigner in the world who knows this location!"

A last minute visit to Bangkok's new Suvanabhumi Airport was planned in time for the King of Thailand's birthday. Ironically, I was already there! Families brought their children and cars lined the parkway entering the airport. Security failed to move anyone. After getting into position through unknown grounds and fencing, we were lucky to find the perfect location and filmed the best moments of the Super Jumbo moving in and out of the specially built Thai Airways hangar. The plane displayed a special decal of the King's crest. The final preparations and takeoff were filmed against the backdrop of the newest airport in Asia, the aircraft and airport like two trophies of equal caliber! Now came one of my biggest challenges—getting the proper permissions to film in my home country, the United States.

Upon hearing the plans for the long-awaited United States tour, my excitement was equal to my fear of not succeeding. First, this was post 9/11, and freelancing was nearly impossible. Second, two A380s were coming, one landing in New York and one in Los Angeles—at the same time. And finally, we had no idea until the last minute if we would receive permission. With nearly three dozen emails to different parties, Lufthansa was unmatched in providing excellent help to our team in New York as well as our West Coast team. This occasion would be unique because Lufthansa was inaugurating the A380's first scheduled passenger flight!

Upon arriving at JFK, we learned that official media passes were necessary—but since I had bombarded Lufthansa Press Relations with emails, they remembered who I was and granted special permission due to our team's world tour efforts. We were again blessed, but not for long; we had missed the press busses to the main ramp to film the first U.S. arrival. Shockingly, so had the Director of Marketing

Taking a break from Abu Dhabi sun, I discuss the next filming sequence in the shadow of an Airbus A300F.

for Lufthansa. Due to this, a CBS crew, my team of two, and the Lufthansa Director were picked up by a security escort and driven over taxiways and runways at speeds exceeding eighty miles per hour! We arrived in time to film a momentous landing on a cold winter day. Had the Lufthansa Marketing Director not also missed the press bus, we would have never made it. Our luck continued.

The press coverage in the States was unmatched. At JFK Airport, the Lufthansa and Airbus team had multiple press conferences including Chief Operating Officer John Leahy, who continued selling the efficiency of the Super Jumbo. Being a part of this experience

was about as close as one can come to a World Cup for aviation!

The highlights during the two years were worth all of the effort. Every accomplishment built momentum. I am not anyone special, just someone who wants to expose aviation to the public and who is blessed by God with the faith to pursue this amazing voyage. In retrospect, we are simply a bunch of volunteers who care very much about aviation!

So going back to the beginning over two years earlier, was that typhoon a problem or a blessing? Was it luck guiding my team, or an angel in the airfield? I do not believe in just luck.

The serene countryside paints a peaceful picture as an A380 prepares to touch down at its home base of Toulouse, France.

FIRST FLIGHTS
AND PRELIMARY TESTS

TOULOUSE

Wednesday, April 27, 2005, was the day Airbus gave birth to a new era in aviation travel. After well over a decade of research, planning, and development, Airbus was finally prepared to show the world its newest gem. The countdown to the first flight of the A380 had commenced when the first aircraft to come off the Jean-Luc Lagardère final assembly line was transferred to the Airbus flight test center on April 6, 2005. During the following weeks the A380 was put through various ground tests by the multinational crew in preparation for its maiden flight. Captained by Claude Lelaie, senior vice president of Airbus Flight Division, and Jacques Rosay, chief test pilot and vice president, the remaining crew consisted of Fernando Alonso, vice president Flight Division, Flight Test Engineering, and flight test engineers Jacky Joye, Manfred Birnfeld, and Gérard Desbois.

On that historic Wednesday, at 10:29 a.m., the Airbus A380-800 (MSN001)—carrying the registration F-WWOW, powered by four Rolls-Royce Trent 900 engines and weighing 421 tonnes (928,146 pounds), the highest ever of any civil airliner to date—took off for its maiden flight on runway 32L, at Toulouse Blagnac International Airport in France.

During the flight, which took the aircraft around South West France, the six crewmembers explored the aircraft's flight envelope. They also tested the A380's handling using both direct and normal flight control laws with the landing gear up and down, and with all flaps' and slats' settings during the part of the flight at cruise altitude. Three hours and 54 minutes later, at 2:23 p.m., the A380 touched back down at the Toulouse airport. The first flight marked the beginning of a flight test program which would involve more than 2,500 hours of test flights on a total of five development aircraft, prior to the certification of the A380 by the European and U.S. airworthiness authorities.

A380 MSN 1 takes off with Toulouse Blagnac International Airport in the background.

Three A380s are nestled together under the hot sun at Airbus' factories where these early test aircraft were assembled.

[above] Getting some attention in front of the A380 final assembly hangars, a future Singapore Airlines aircraft has only its tail painted at this point.

[right] The red tape on the leading edges and the extra protruding sensors on MSN 1 confirm that another successful test flight has just concluded.

An Airbus Beluga Super Transporter on the take-off roll with a future Singapore Airlines A380 in the distance.

It is always a special occasion to catch two active A380s performing flight tests at the same time.

Performing a touch-and-go landing, this A380 is captured near a Northwest A330 and a Lufthansa A340 being prepared for delivery.

FRANKFURT

By Bruno Pinheiro

On Saturday, October 29, 2005, at 8:56 a.m., the A380 (MSN004)—registration F-WWDD—landed on runway 25R at Frankfurt Airport, with a landing weight of 382 tonnes, just 4 tonnes below the maximum. After touchdown the A380 taxied directly to stand E9 at terminal 2. Despite fresh wind, the cool temperatures, and the light mist, thousands of spectators welcomed the A380 on its first airport capability tests.

Frankfurt Airport will eventually have eighteen stands capable of handling the A380. At a width of 80 meters (262.5 feet), stand E9—where the A380 carried out its tests—is an International Civil Aviation Organization (ICAO) Code F stand, capable of accommodating any aircraft with a wingspan of 80 meters. Code F stands are also capable of handling multi-aircraft ramp usage (MARS). This allows two single-aisle aircraft to be parked in the same stand as the A380. Code E stands, which are 65 meters (213.3 feet) wide, can also handle the A380, if the size of the aircraft on adjacent stands is limited to that of smaller widebodies.

The Frankfurt Airport check exercises represented the culmination of many years of cooperation between Airbus and the airport community. During its "working visit" the A380 tests were conducted with the assistance of Lufthansa and the aircraft was put through various ground tests. Several ramp scenarios were simulated. These included a full ground support equipment positioning, passenger bridge testing, cargo loading and offloading, fuel bowser testing, catering, firefighting, and de-icing. In total over forty different ground support equipment (GSE) were used, twice the number usually needed for a standard A380 or B747.

Following the compatibility tests, the aircraft was towed to a Lufthansa hangar for an evening event and was then towed around the airport for six hours for instrument landing system (ILS) tests. The following day the A380 returned to its home base in southern France.

A wide perspective showing the activity around the A380 at the special gate reserved for airport compatibility tests.

Frankfurt Airport saw the first use of these interesting testing vehicles that measured the dimensions of the mega airliner as it parked at its new gate.

A close-up view of the testing demonstrates the measuring devices at work.

A misty, early morning 9 a.m. departure ended the first ever trip of the A380 to an international airport.

On November 10, 2005, the Airbus A380 (MSN 001)—decorated with a Singapore Airlines logo, carrying the registration F-WWOW, and powered by four Rolls Royce Trent 900 engines—took off from Toulouse, France, at 12:20 p.m. for a nine-day Asia-Pacific tour, marking the first time the aircraft was seen outside Europe.

During its tour the aircraft visited Singapore, Australia, and Malaysia. The nine-day trip gave customers Singapore Airlines, Qantas, and Malaysian Airlines the chance to see the aircraft before the first deliveries, while also allowing airports to test equipment and demonstrate their readiness for the A380's entry into commercial service.

The first stop on the tour was Singapore on November 11, where some minor testing was carried out including airside checks on taxiways and runways, along with bridge positioning checks on gate F31. It was then flown to Brisbane,

Australia, where Qantas logo decals were applied before the aircraft flew over the Gold Coast. During its visit to Brisbane the A380 also performed airside tests on runways and taxiways.

The following day the A380 made its next stop at Sydney (Kingsford Smith) International Airport. GSE trials were performed at the Qantas Jet Base. Equipment successfully tested included upper deck catering vehicle prototypes, stairs, cargo loaders, air conditioning units, and the ground power unit (GPU). The A380 also performed a flying display over the Sydney Harbor with thousands of spectators present.

The next day the aircraft traveled to Melbourne for further compatibility testing. Particular attention was paid to bridge positioning tests on Melbourne Airport's gate 9. Melbourne was the first airport in Australia with upper deck bridge capability and the tests proved the aircraft was easily accessible for passengers and crew.

The historic first ever arrival in Asia at Singapore Changi Airport. Singapore Airlines announces to the world that it will be the first to fly the A380 in regular passenger service.

[above] Changi's impressive control tower closely monitors the first A380's progress around the airport's taxiways.

[left] Airport compatibility tests were an important part of this first Asian tour. MSN 1 is seen here approaching the gate in Singapore for the first time.

Moments after gently touching down in Sydney for the first time, MSN 1 rolls out with thrust reversers deployed.

The A380 is seen here being towed minutes after emerging from its secluded overnight parking bay. The crew and passengers of a Qantas A330 get a close-up view.

An Air Tahiti Nui A340 shows off its dramatic livery as A380 MSN 1 is readied for its departure.

As a sign of the status granted to this special aircraft, the A380 was given special authority to backtrack along the complete length of the runway before departing Sydney (Kingsford Smith) International Airport.

A380 with the beautiful backdrop of Kuala Lumpur International Airport in Sepang.

With an arrival fit for a king, F-WWOW taxies in to the welcoming sounds of local dancing and music.

[above] A "water gun salute" is a testimony to the importance of the A380 to the people of Malaysia.

[right] An Airbus representative passionately provides facts and history about this groundbreaking aircraft to the VIPs and attending camera crew.

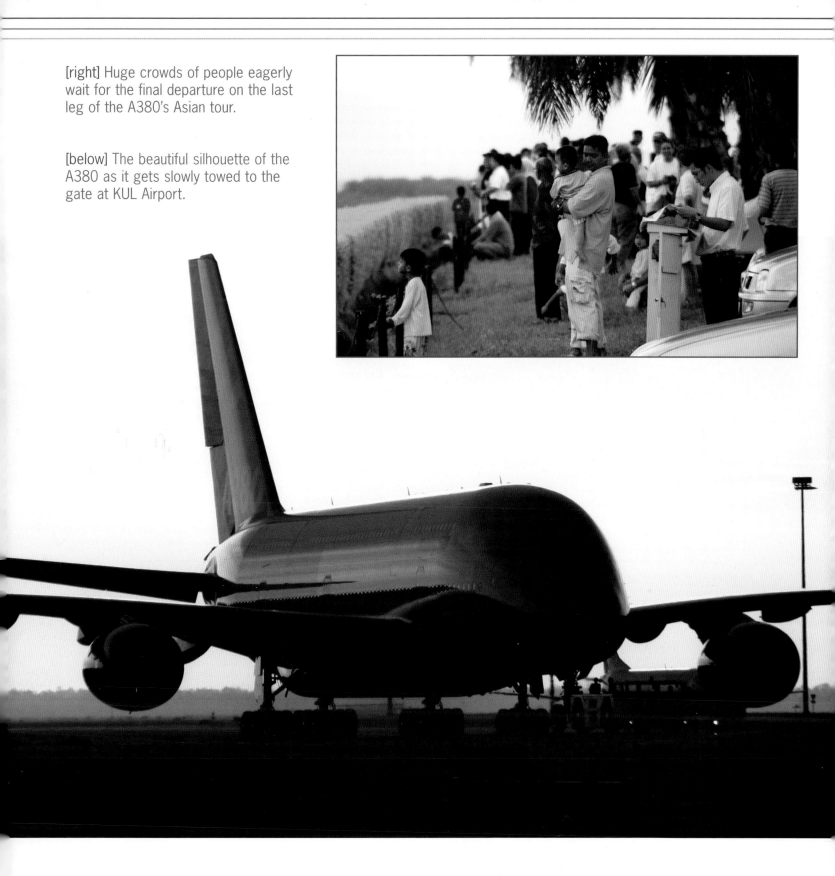

[right] Huge crowds of people eagerly wait for the final departure on the last leg of the A380's Asian tour.

[below] The beautiful silhouette of the A380 as it gets slowly towed to the gate at KUL Airport.

[above] MSN 1 starts
its final take-off run from
Kuala Lumpur
International Airport.

[right] One of the four Rolls
Royce Trent 900 engines
that power the A380.

[right] A surprise return flyby over the airport was a great sign of respect to the Malaysian people and was welcomed by all in attendance.

[below] Liftoff for MSN 1, now on its way back to Toulouse.

COLOMBIA

The Airbus A380 (MSN 004), carrying the registration F- WWDD, opted for Jose Maria Cordova Airport in Colombia, to perform its high altitude tests. The aircraft flew from its base in Toulouse on January 10, 2006, and flew directly to Medellin, Colombia, which is located in a small valley at an altitude of about 2,133 meters (7,000 feet).

With a team of thirty-five engineers and flight crewmembers, various tests were carried out between January 11 and 13 to determine how the aircraft would perform at high altitude airports. The aim of such trials is to validate full functionality of engines, systems, and materials under difficult conditions. The aircraft's four Rolls Royce Trent 900 engines were tested up to their maximum thrust and the aircraft successfully performed six takeoffs. The flights also provided the opportunity to test autopilot landings at high altitude airports. The auxiliary power unit (APU), which provides electrical and pneumatic power when the aircraft is on the ground before the main engines start, was also comprehensively tested to verify its performance at high altitude with maximum load conditions.

Following the Medellin tests the aircraft flew to Pointe-à-Pitre, Guadeloupe, for two days where it performed similar engine tests, including two takeoffs at an altitude just above sea level.

A380 (MSN 004) brakes gracefully during its first arrival in South America at Medellin, Colombia.

Keeping cool! A seldom seen sight was the A380 with all sixteen passenger doors open at the same time.

Airbus A380 (MSN 004) with Rolls Royce powered Trent 900 engines and carrying the registration F-WWDD, was put to its first extreme low temperatures test at Iqaluit, Canada, between February 6 and 10, 2006.

During the five days of cold weather testing the A380, along with fifty engineers and flight test crewmembers, experienced temperatures of –30 degrees Celsius. Due to the extremely cold conditions in Iqaluit, the team consisted of two groups that worked four-hour rotating shifts to limit their exposure to the cold. On the second day of testing the A380 experienced a blizzard, with temperatures dropping to around –50 degrees Celsius including the wind chill factor.

The aim of the tests was to prove the full functionality of the systems under extreme weather conditions. After a full twelve-hour period of low temperatures, the A380's engines and hydraulic systems were powered up. On its way back to home base in Toulouse, France, the A380 also carried out polar navigation tests.

The aircraft's first arrival in Iqaluit, Canada, was an impressive sight—an all white aircraft landing in the Great White North!

"Ice Station Iqaluit"—a term well defined by the arctic climate.

[above] A hot takeoff in the ice-cold Arctic was just another day's work during the long testing schedule of MSN 004.

[right] A frozen, all white F-WWDD is brought to life in frigid –45 degree Celsius temperature.

The wheels supporting the aircraft on the icy and snow covered tarmac of Iqaluit Airport.

A close-up view of the engines and aircraft being warmed up prior to the flight back to Toulouse.

An impressive engine start was witnessed, considering the Arctic sub-zero temperature.

The distant February light started to fade by 3:00 p.m. every day due to Iqaluit's isolated location at the top of the world.

Rolling for takeoff under the crisp, clear Arctic sky.

The size of the A380 is aptly demonstrated here, as it dwarfs Iqaluit's terminal building and main ramp area.

LONDON HEATHROW

The Airbus A380 celebrated its first flight into the United Kingdom on May 18, when it flew over the Airbus U.K. sites of Broughton and Filton as a tribute to the Airbus employees before making its way to London. With gusting crosswinds, the A380 (MSN 004), carrying the registration F-WWDD, made a smoky landing on runway 27L at London Heathrow Airport.

The A380's visit marked the official opening of the new pier 6 at terminal 3, which had been built to accommodate the new aircraft. The 280-meter-long (918 feet), three-story-high pier has aircraft stands to accommodate up to four A380s at a time, two airbridges, and four gate rooms that together seat 2,200 passengers. London Heathrow Airport is likely to be the first European destination when the A380 enters commercial service, and ten carriers have already indicated their intention to operate there.

During its visit at Heathrow, the A380 performed a series of ground handling and compatibility checks in conjunction with airport operator British Airports Authority (BAA), before returning to Berlin to perform alongside the A318 and the A340-600 in the flight displays at the Berlin Air Show International Aerospace Exhibition (ILA).

A historic view as A380 F-WWDD taxis for the first time at London Heathrow Airport with numerous British Airways aircraft in attendance.

One of the most striking angles in which to capture the A380 due to its large contoured and shapely wings.

[right] Impressive in its newness, the massive size of the front landing gear is clearly apparent, with these ground technicians helping to provide perspective.

[below] The Roll Royce Trent 900 engines are engineering masterpieces with four examples powering the A380 over eight thousand miles.

As with other test airports such as Frankfurt, specialized testing equipment is used to determine aircraft clearances in the gate area.

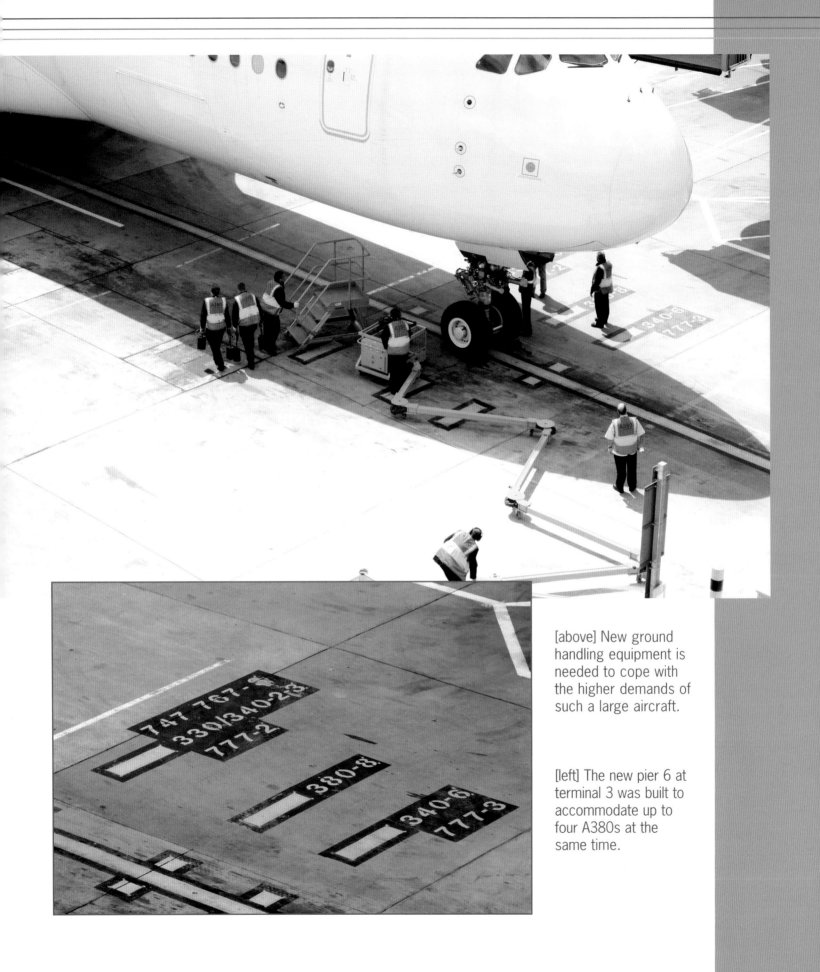

[above] New ground handling equipment is needed to cope with the higher demands of such a large aircraft.

[left] The new pier 6 at terminal 3 was built to accommodate up to four A380s at the same time.

The Union Jack is proudly waved as the A380 taxis on UK soil for the first time

[above] Many people took the time to pay this special guest a visit during the aircraft's first call at Heathrow Airport.

[right] A detailed view of the Trent 900 engine shows the pylon and the attachment point to the wing.

Only one of the two loading bridges is being used.

The power of the Rolls Royce engines is apparent in this dramatic, dusty takeoff as A380 F-WWDD departs from Al Ain's desert runway, a secluded airport in the United Arab Emirates (UAE).

Great nose-on view showing the immense wingspan of this giant aircraft.

[above] MSN 004 during final preparations before departing later in the evening to Toulouse after completing six days of testing in the Emirate of Abu Dhabi.

[right] The complexity of the A380 is more apparent the closer one gets to the aircraft.

F-WWDD is seen departing on a test flight after baking in the 45 degree Celsius (113 degree Fahrenheit) sun for several hours.

Fully fuelled and ready to depart back to France, F-WWDD makes its way to the active runway.

The elevation of Al Ain International Airport's runway is obvious in this ominous head on view of MSN 004 taxiing for takeoff.

[right] MSN 004 basks in the intense Al Ain sun between flight tests.

[below] This wide angle view from behind demonstrates the ramp space needed to park an A380.

ADDIS ABABA

The Airbus A380 (MSN 009), carrying the registration F-WWEA and powered by Engine Alliance GP7200, visited Bole International Airport in Addis Ababa, Ethiopia, on October 16, 2006. Located at an altitude of 2,325 meters (7,627 feet) above sea level, the A380 carried out further high altitude and hot weather tests. A380 (MSN 009) then made its way to Al Ain, United Arab Emirates, for further testing.

First arrival at Addis Ababa in the shadow of a striking Ethiopian mountain range.

A380 (MSN 009) taxis to a warm welcome on the apron of Bole International Airport.

[top right] Excited activity surrounds MSN 009 after its first arrival in Africa.

[above] An Airbus security personnel talks to a VIP in this wide angle view of F-WWEA.

A tired crew rests between VIP visitors after the long flight from France.

The Ethiopian flag is proudly displayed from a cockpit window of MSN 009.

Everybody was in awe during the first public appearance of the Super Jumbo. MSN 1 can be seen standing proud in front of thousands of admiring Paris Air Show spectators.

AIR SHOWS
AND VIP TOURS

THE 46TH INTERNATIONAL PARIS AIR SHOW, LE BOURGET—JUNE 2005

By Bruno Pinheiro

The Airbus A3XX project was first showcased to the public at the 42nd Paris Air Show, Le Bourget, in 1997. Eight years later and having completed just under two months of flight-testing since its maiden flight, the A380 made its air show debut at Le Bourget with a seven-minute flying display during each day of the show and in the company of the smallest and the longest aircraft of the Airbus family, the A318 and the A340-600, respectively.

Held between June 13 and 19 in 2005, the 46th Paris Air Show, Le Bourget, broke attendance records and proved to be the most successful air show to date. With Airbus Chief Test Pilot Jacques Rosay and Captain Wolfgang Absmeier at the controls, the Rolls-Royce Trent 900 powered A380 performed a routine display highlighting the maneuverability and quietness of the A380. Packed with instrumentation and water ballast tanks on both passenger decks, the A380 performed various maneuvers including a slow flyby, which saw the aircraft pass down the runway at around 220 kilometers per hour (120 knots) at 245 meters (800 feet).

A detailed model displayed in the interior exhibit of the European Aeronautic Defence and Space Company (EADS) helped show off the A380 future interior to visitors, who then could step outside to witness the actual aircraft for the first time.

A380 MSN 1 is nicely framed by Airbus' A340-600 as it is prepared for its first ever public aerial display.

[above] History was made as the first ever liftoff of the A380 at the Paris Air Show was captured to a chorus of "oohs" and "aahs!"

[right] Airbus proudly displayed the insignias of all A380 customers who had committed to operating the world's largest commercial airline.

[left] Steep climb out . . .

[below] Sharp turn . . .

Banking in front of the crowd . . .

And another slow-speed flyby. The A380 kept its landing gear down throughout its flying displays at the Paris Air Show, only cycling them up after a final flyby on Sunday as it flew back to Toulouse. Putting the landing gear up had been done before in some brief testing, but not in public.

The appearance of the Airbus A380 was the high-light of the ninth Dubai Air Show, held between November 20 and 24, 2005, in the United Arab Emirates. It displays the full Emirates livery with Emirates colors on the tail, and the word "Emirates" on a bright red background on its belly.

Despite its appearance the A380 was not painted in Emirates colors. Due to the A380's tight certification schedule, painting the aircraft would prove to be too time consuming. Instead, a full customization was done with removable decals. This technique was also applied to the airframe (of MSN 001) that performed the Asian-Pacific tour the previous week.

The Airbus A380 (MSN 004)—carrying the registration F-WWDD, and also referred to as the "empress of the skies," during the Dubai Air Show—arrived on Friday, November 18. The appearance of the A380 at the Dubai Air Show marked the first time that the A380 participated in an air show outside of Europe, and the home of Emirates, the largest customer for the A380 with forty-three frames on order and an additional two leased via the leasing company ILFC. The Dubai Air Show was also an opportunity for Middle East A380 customers to go onboard and see the aircraft firsthand.

During the air show the A380 performed a flying display every afternoon. Under the blinding sun, crowds of people came out to see the A380 performing steep climbs, sharp turns, and low speed flybys. It also demonstrated its maneuver-ability and quietness before it landed and closed the flight display for the day.

Airbus A380 (MSN 004) is seen making its first spectacular flying display in the clear blue skies of Dubai. This was the first time an A380 was seen in an airline's full livery, albeit just in decal form.

Close-up of the nose section and the mighty tug that is required to maneuver this immense aircraft.

Airbus A380 F-WWDD banks sharply after takeoff at the start of its flying display.

[above] Takeoff shot illustrating the wing-mounted outer main landing gear leaving the runway ahead of the center gear.

[left] With Emirates being the largest customer to date for the A380, this will soon be a common sight at airports around the world.

With slats and flaps extended, F-WWDD makes a dazzling slow speed flyby.

This series of photos demonstrates a full turn in front of the crowds of impressed observers.

The A380's fly-by-wire system safely allows this type of low-altitude handling.

The huge Emirates logo will even be visible from cruising altitudes!

A great angle showing the details of the many control surfaces on the underside of MSN 004.

[above] The Airbus flight crew was always available to discuss the A380 systems and controls to pilots, potential customers, and media personnel.

[left] A smooth landing ends yet another successful flying display.

The Airbus A380 SuperJumbo was the star guest at the Asian Aerospace 2006 air show held at Changi, Singapore, from February 21 to 22. The biennial event, which is the third biggest air show in the world with only Paris and Farnborough ahead of it, was host to over nine hundred and forty exhibitors, from forty-three countries, and with announcements of record deals in excess of $15 billion—four and a half times the amount recorded in its 2004 event. The air show was also attended by 153 delegations from forty-four countries and over 34,300 trade participants from eighty-nine countries. During the four-day event over sixty thousand visitors were curious to spot the A380 and see it perform its famous flying displays.

Unlike its first visit to Changi in November 2005, the A380 appeared in full Singapore Airlines livery. Singapore Airlines is the launch customer for the A380-800 and is expected to take delivery of its first of nineteen airframes on order from October 2007. To apply the Singapore livery on the A380, a team of 110 people worked for fifty-four hours within a three-day slot to apply removable decals prior to the aircraft leaving Toulouse for Singapore.

In total, between 1,100 and 1,200 square meters of decals were used, representing about 1,200 individual decals. A varnish was also applied over the decals to ensure they would stay in place during flight and to round off the edges, which maintains the aircraft's aerodynamics.

With Pilot Peter Chandler at the controls of the Rolls Royce Trent 900 powered A380 SuperJumbo (MSN 004), carrying the registration F-WWDD, performed a routine flying display, similar to those seen at the Paris and Dubai Air Shows. During the event the A380 also performed several airport compatibility tests to allow the Changi Airport ground staff members to familiarize themselves with the handling of the A380.

A380 (MSN 004) made its debut at Asian Aerospace 2006 in full Singapore Airlines colors.

[left] Singapore Airlines proudly reminded all visitors that it will be the "First to Fly the A380."

[below] Helping to give scale to the size of this aircraft, F-WWDD is captured crossing the bridge at Changi Airport.

On the ramp and open for VIP tours as MSN 004 rests between flying displays.

[left] The A380, in any form, draws crowds of fans wherever it is!

[below] The impressive EADS/Airbus display inside the Changi International Exhibition and Convention Center.

[right] The flying display was a crowd favorite as the plane performed at extremely low altitude on this cloudy and extremely humid day.

[below] The highly advanced Airbus fly-by-wire system allows for slow and spectacular near-stall passes, as pictured here.

An excellent view showing off the huge flaps during the aerial display.

BERLIN AIR SHOW ILA

The Airbus A380 was the highlight of the Berlin Air Show ILA, held on the southern section of Berlin-Schönefeld Airport, in Germany between May 16 and 21, 2006. The Berlin Air Show ILA is the oldest aviation show in the world and ranks among the world's largest and most important aerospace exhibitions. Held biennially, the ILA 2006 was attended by over 250,000 visitors, including 115,000 trade visitors, and also featured 340 aircraft on display. Additionally, it was the A380's first visit to ILA that helped break attendance records and make it the most successful exhibition to date.

During the six-day event, the A380 performed a routine flying display alongside the smallest and the longest aircraft of the Airbus family, the A318 and the A340-600, respectively. The A380 (MSN 004), carrying the registration F-WWDD, displayed Lufthansa decals on the front of the fuselage. Lufthansa is one of the launch customers for the A380 and the largest European customer, with a firm order for fifteen frames, and is expected to take delivery of its first aircraft in the summer of 2009.

This view helps capture the incredible interest, rain or shine, that this aircraft garners as it is presented to audiences around the world. German pride in the A380 program was very apparent at ILA Berlin 2006.

A view showing the Lufthansa decals added after MSN 004's testing session at London Heathrow Airport.

The flying demonstration has been the highlight of the day at every air show the A380 has attended.

F-WWDD appears to be following a much smaller flying object during the course of its aerial display.

FARNBOROUGH AIR SHOW

The Airbus A380 SuperJumbo was the star of the 45th Farnborough International Air Show, held in England, between July 17 and 23, 2006. Located thirty miles southwest of London, the seven-day, biennial international trade fair for the aerospace business, ranks among the most important air shows in the industry in terms of exhibitors and attendance. During the show, a total of $42 billion worth of deals were announced and more than 270,000 trade and public visitors attended the show, making it the most successful Farnborough Air Show in history.

The highlight of the air show was the daily flying display of the Airbus A380 (MSN 001) powered by four Rolls Royce Trent 900 engines. While similar flying displays had been seen with previous air shows that the A380 had attended, it was the flying display with the Red Arrows that made the Airbus A380 first visit to Farnborough memorable. The A380, in formation with the Red Arrows, flew at about 300–320 knots over Farnborough. To perform the flight, the A380 crew and the aerobatic team had to agree not only on the flight formation, but also on issues such as radio frequencies and safety procedures. The flying display demonstrated that despite the size of the A380 it still remained a very maneuverable aircraft both on the ground and in the air.

A historic flyby with the Red Arrows was the surprise highlight of Farnborough 2006.

Farnborough offered some of the best, unobstructed views available of the A380 than at any air show in the world.

A majestic and very quiet liftoff at Farnborough 2006.

A spectacularly slow flyby allows the crowds a clear view of the landing gear being raised.

MSN 001 sits near the Airbus chalet ready for its next flying display.

A steep yet gracious turn as MSN 001 heads back toward the crowds for yet another pass.

F-WWOW preparing to touch down in front of its smaller stable mate, the A340-600 that is about to depart.

A successful end to the day's flying display as MSN 001 lands in front of thousands of satisfied spectators.

A panoramic view of an Etihad-decaled A380 at Abu Dhabi International Airport during the first VIP visit to this Emirate.

This was a rare opportunity to capture the A380 flying low and slow over a major city. Here one sees F-WWDD flying parallel to famous Cornish Road in Abu Dhabi on its way over the Emirates Palace Hotel on a hot and hazy afternoon.

[above] The red carpet treatment was extended to VIPs, as well as the A380 itself, on arrival at Abu Dhabi Airport for a brief one-day visit for Etihad Airways and its employees.

[right] The beauty of the A380's sleek contoured wing is highlighted by a row of palm trees in the background.

Spectacular two-story view from the front door of MSN 004 looking down on the very exclusive VIP lounge at Abu Dhabi International Airport.

[above] An Airbus test pilot explains the details of the cockpit to visiting VIPs. Note the effectiveness of the orange glare screens that offer a clear view of the A340-500 parked just in front of the A380, which would otherwise be invisible.

[left] The electrifying flyby past down Abu Dhabi's main runway marks the start of this VIP visit.

[above] The extra wide staircase going to the upper deck allows two people to stand side by side or to pass each other on the way up or down.

[left] An "in-your-face" view of the gigantic landing gear overshadowing even the tallest ground crew.

[below] A passenger view of the engines as seen from inside the aircraft, with the Etihad falcon symbol looking particularly stately in this photograph.

BANGKOK—VIP VISIT

The Airbus A380 SuperJumbo made a special visit to Bangkok's Suvarnabhumi Airport on December 5, 2006, as part of the commemoration of the seventy-ninth birthday of His Majesty King Bhumibol Adulyadej (Rama IX), the King of Thailand.

Captained by Lucien Beinard, the Rolls Royce powered A380 (MSN 002), carrying the registration F-WXXL, landed at 1:22 p.m. for its first visit to the Kingdom of Thailand, following an eleven-hour and thirty-five-minute flight from Toulouse, France. The A380 appeared with a special King Symbol on the side of the fuselage.

During the visit the A380 was presented to officials from Thai Airways International and the Airport Authority of Thailand, and undertook a series of airport compatibility verification tests. Bangkok is the home of Thai Airways International, which has a firm order for six frames, with deliveries expected to commence in 2011. The airline plans to deploy the A380 on popular routes from Bangkok to Frankfurt, London, and Paris.

A night shot into the giant Thai Airways hangar, where four A380s can be parked simultaneously. A decal of the King's crest was applied to the front of the plane for the following day's ceremonies.

F-WWXL pictured beside a Thai Airways A340-500.

[above] MSN 002 undergoing final preparations before departing for France.

[right] The King's crest was affixed while in Bangkok, but it was removed before departure at the end of its brief two-day stay.

F-WWXL starting its take-off roll at Bangkok's new Suvarnabhumi Airport, with the stunning terminal buildings visible in the background.

BEHIND THE SCENES

[above] Testing was one of the main functions of this trip to Abu Dhabi. This engine pylon was loaded with test sensors to collect data.

[right] Technicians busy at work inside MSN 004 at Abu Dhabi Airport.

Countless tests performed by the engineers and computers throughout the test period lead to the type's certification in December 2006.

Never-ending rows of computers and monitors often lined both decks of MSN 001 and MSN 004.

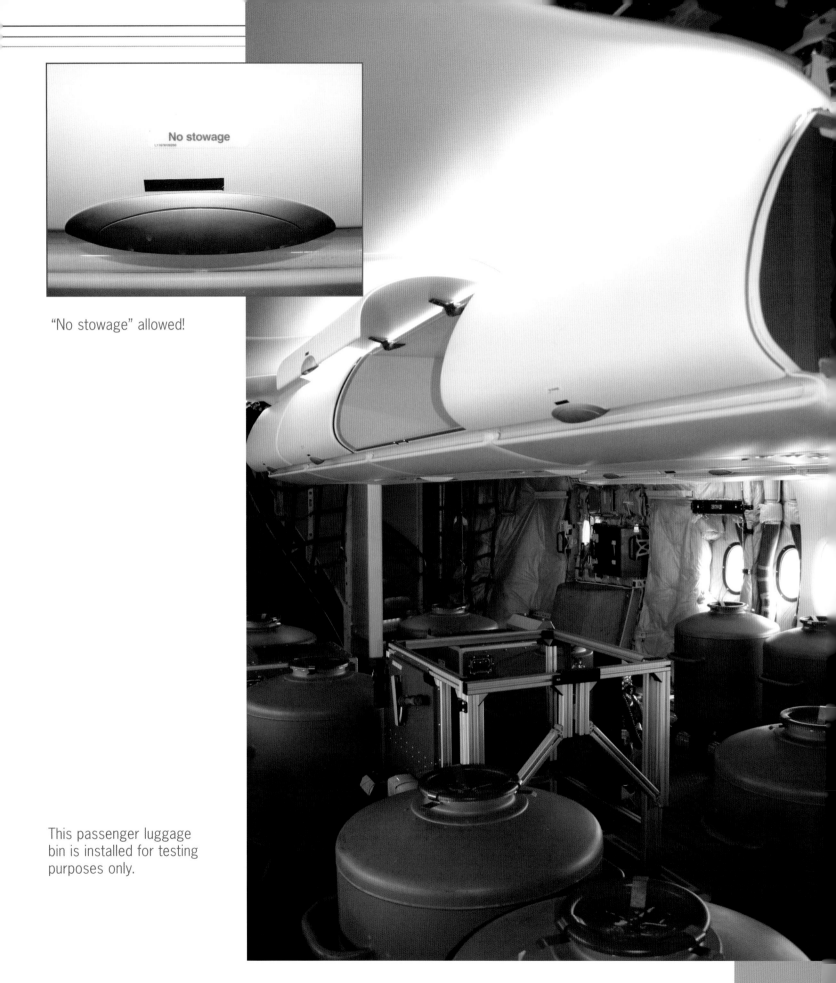

No stowage

"No stowage" allowed!

This passenger luggage bin is installed for testing purposes only.

A camera closely monitors the wing, collecting valuable in-flight test information.

The new terminal that will accommodate the A380 when it enters service is seen behind two Orient Thai Boeing 747s.

FINAL TESTS AND PASSENGER FLIGHTS

SEOUL, SOUTH KOREA—GLOBAL ROUTE PROVING

The Airbus A380 (MSN 002), carrying the registration F-WXXL and powered by four Rolls Royce Trent 900 engines, started its technical route proving exercise on November 13, 2006, to carry out function and reliability tests at key airports around the world. Starting from Toulouse, France, the aircraft visited ten different airports in four trips. These included Singapore and Seoul, Korea, during the first trip (November 14 and 15), then Hong Kong, China, and Narita, Japan (November 18 and 19). The third trip brought the aircraft to Guangzhou (November 22), and Beijing and Shanghai (November 23) in China. The fourth and final trip took the A380 around the globe, via both North and South Poles. It visited Johannesburg, South Africa (November 26), Sydney, Australia (November 28), and Vancouver, Canada (November 29), prior to returning to Toulouse.

The technical route proving exercise trials are required for Type Certification, by the Airworthiness Authorities European Aviation Safety Agency (EASA) and the Federal Aviation Administration (FAA). The trials had to be carried out with over 150 flight hours on a continuous typical airline schedule, while the aircraft performed in its normal operational environment.

TOKYO, JAPAN

The Airbus A380 (MSN 002), carrying the registration F-WXXL, arrived at Tokyo Narita International Airport, Japan, on November 19, 2006, as part of a final series of test flights intended for the SuperJumbo's air worthiness certification by EASA and FAA.

This was the first time that the A380 visited Japan. With the stop over in Narita, the aircraft underwent several routine ground handling tests, which included such work as maintenance, fueling, and the use of boarding bridges. Despite the A380 not having gathered any orders from Japanese airlines, Japan expects regular visits by the A380. The airport exercises and tests carried out will help airport officials plan for the regular service of the A380 in Narita, with several A380 customers already indicating their intention to operate in the airport in the future.

On November 20, 2006, the A380 returned to Toulouse for its preparation for the third proving exercises that would take the A380 to Chinese airports in Beijing, Shanghai, and Guangdong.

A380 (MSN 002) approaches Tokyo Narita International Airport in dark overcast conditions.

First A380 touchdown in Japan!

F-WXXL arriving at its gate for tests in preparation for the type's entry into service.

GUANGZHOU, CHINA

On the third set of proving exercises the Airbus A380 (MSN 002), carrying the registration F-WXXL, made its first visit to mainland China, on Wednesday, November 22, 2006, when it arrived at Guangzhou's Baiyun International Airport, the capital of South China's Guangdong Province. During its visit to China the A380 also visited Beijing and Shanghai.

Guangzhou is home to China Southern Airlines, the only current Chinese customer for the A380, with five frames on firm orders. The big-city markets of Shanghai, Beijing, and Guangzhou are seen as ready-made for the A380 because of their massive populations. With demand over the next twenty years estimated at 2,900 new planes of various sizes worth $280 billion—around 10 percent of estimated global demand over that period—China represents one of the holy grails in terms of aircraft sales.

Baiyun International Airport welcomes the A380 on a quick stopover before MSN 002 departs for Beijing.

Short taxi following the test flight's arrival at Guangzhou.

Airbus engineers
work on the
A380 before its
next flight.

BEIJING, CHINA

On November 23, 2006, the Airbus A380 SuperJumbo made its way to Beijing Capital International Airport following a flight from Guangzhou. Currently, only four airports in China have runways that can accommodate the A380—namely, Beijing, Shanghai, Guangzhou, and Hong Kong.

In the north of new terminal 3 of Beijing Capital International Airport, Ameco is currently building the largest hangar in Asia, which will be capable of handling the A380. The total building area is 70,437 square meters, and the total investment for construction is RMB 700 million. Once completed, the hangar will be capable of offering maintenance work for the A380.

The impressive VIP center at Beijing Airport welcomes A380 SuperJumbo F-WXXL.

[above] A close-up view of VIPs visiting the first A380 in Beijing. China is considered to be a large future market for this extra large airliner.

[left] The notorious Beijing air partly obscures a busy ramp scene as the A380 prepares for departure. Next stop: Shanghai!

After being towed to the runway, MSN 002 performs its engine start-up sequence for a 6:00 p.m. departure.

Lining up for takeoff to Shanghai.

JOHANNESBURG, SOUTH AFRICA

The Airbus A380 SuperJumbo arrived at Johannesburg, South Africa, on November 26, 2006. During its first visit to South Africa, the aircraft carried out a series of auto-land operations, showing the aircraft's ability to perform fully automatic landings. The major highlight of the exercise at Johannesburg was the A380's capability to fly ultra long-range routes at maximum payload. The A380 departed Johannesburg, South Africa, from runway 03L, with its maximum take-off weight of 555 tonnes (1,223,565 pounds) the heaviest aircraft ever to take off from O. R. Tambo International Airport, located at 1,680 meters (5,323 feet) above sea level.

From Johannesburg, the A380 flew nonstop to Sydney, making a South Pole crossing. The aircraft landed at Sydney airport after a flight of around sixteen hours covering a distance of 13,512 kilometers (7,296 nautical miles). This trial demonstrated the A380's excellent performance at high altitude airports.

F-WXXL about to touch down in South Africa for the first time.

Following a flight of fourteen hours and twenty-five minutes across the Pacific from Sydney, Australia, the Airbus A380 arrived at YVR Vancouver International Airport, Canada, at 7:32 a.m. on November 29, 2006. Scheduled to arrive at 7:30 a.m., the flight was running 15 minutes ahead of schedule, but the flight crew delayed the landing to give the hundreds of viewers and photographers better light.

During its visit to the only North American stop for the A380 during the route proving in YVR Vancouver, the A380 was serviced and re-fuelled. It was also visited by a number of groups, among them representatives from YVR, airlines, and ground handlers.

The A380 departed snowy YVR Vancouver at 4:30 p.m. The trip from Vancouver via the North Pole to Toulouse marked the end of a series of eighteen-day-stretch, technical, route-proving flights for the A380, the final process in a long test flight program that began in April 2005.

MSN 002 taxis to the gate at a cold Vancouver airport.

On March 20, 2007, the Australian airline Qantas (Queensland and Northern Territory Aerial Service), in collaboration with Los Angeles International Airport (LAX) authorities, initiated its first route proving flight with an A380 (MSN 001) from Toulouse, France, to LAX. Qantas Airways is the second largest customer for the A380-800, with a firm order for twenty frames. During the route proving exercise, the A380 also underwent airport compatibility tests, which included fueling, airfield maneuvering, docking at the terminal gate, ground handling services, and equipment.

On Monday, March 19, 2007, the Airbus A380 operated by Qantas touched down at LAX at 9:30 a.m. on runway 24R. After it touched down, the Airbus A380 SuperJumbo taxied to the Imperial Terminal on the airport's south side,

where it received a warm welcome from the thousands of spectators who were eager to capture one of the first landings of the A380s on U.S. soil. The A380 (MSN 001) carried several dozen crewmembers and technicians, as well as banks of instruments and water tanks designed to shift the plane's center of gravity in flight.

Just a few minutes earlier, another A380 (MSN 007) being operated by German airline Lufthansa, with its own route proving exercises, landed at John F. Kennedy International Airport (JFK), New York, after a flight from Frankfurt, Germany, with some five hundred passengers onboard.

After a two-day visit the Airbus A380 SuperJumbo departed LAX at 6:20 p.m. on runway 25R for a flight back to home base in Toulouse, France.

The A380 taxis in front of the famous Theme Building at LAX before departing back to Toulouse.

[above] A wide-angle view showing off the impressive dimensions of the A380 sitting on the ramp.

[left] Everyone at this event, including these Swissport ground personnel, was in good spirits and eagerly welcomed the A380 to LAX airport.

High security surrounded MSN 001's first visit to LAX.

[left] The A380 departs into the dark stormy sky for its long eleven-hour flight back to Toulouse.

[below] A nice size comparison between the original "Queen of the Skies" and the new SuperJumbo at a busy LAX.

LUFTHANSA ROUTE PROVING

On March 19, 2007, Lufthansa—the largest European customer for the Airbus A380 SuperJumbo with fifteen frames on order—initiated series of route proving exercises in collaboration with Airbus. In total the Rolls Royce Trent 900 powered Airbus A380-800 (MSN 007), carrying the registration F-WWJB, flew more than sixty-five hours over a distance of sixty thousand kilometers on its route from Frankfurt to New York, Chicago, Hong Kong, and Washington,

D.C. In all 3,750 passengers, primarily consisting of Airbus and Lufthansa staff and guests, had the opportunity to experience traveling in the Airbus A380. The main impression among the passengers was the feeling of a light, airy, and spacious cabin. The passengers were also amazed at how quiet the cabin of the A380 was during both takeoff and cruising. While the passengers were impressed with the cabin improvements over existing aircraft, the Lufthansa flight crewmembers were impressed by

Lufthansa initiated its passenger route proving flights from its base in Frankfurt, seen here as MSN 007 pushes back for one of the four flights.

the aircraft's maneuverability and performance.

The route proving exercise was the third time in which Lufthansa was an exclusive partner with Airbus on the A380 program. In March 2006 Lufthansa cabin crew was involved in the evacuation test, and in September 2006, Lufthansa cabin crew also helped conduct the first A380 early long flights (ELF).

On March 19, A380 (MSN 007) made its first landing on U.S. soil when it landed on runway 22L at John F. Kennedy International Airport, New York, after a flight from Frankfurt, Germany, with some five hundred passengers onboard. It coincided with A380 (MSN 001) landing at LAX.

On March 23, the A380 arrived at Hong Kong International Airport after an overnight flight from Frankfurt. Later in the afternoon the Airbus A380 performed a demo flight for the Asian media. During the flight that lasted one hour and a half, journalists had the opportunity to experience the A380 for the first time. The general consensus among the journalists was once again the quietness, spaciousness, and comfort of the A380 cabin.

Marking the very first arrival in the United States, MSN 007 entered the aviation history books when it touched down on U.S. soil.

[left] Rolling to a stop seconds after touch-down between snow-covered fields.

[below] MSN 007 is patriotically flying the flag of the United States of America after landing at New York's JFK airport for the first time.

No American passenger-carrying airline had ordered the A380 at the time of this U.S. tour.

[above] F-WWJB is tucked away overnight in a secluded and secure part of JFK.

[right] Comfort is obviously the ultimate goal and a major selling point of the A380.

[above] A view of the spacious upper-deck business class layout is provided by Airbus and Lufthansa for this series of route proving flights.

[left] A sign of luxury, this softly lit spiral staircase leads to the upper deck at the rear of the aircraft.

This section of MSN 007 has an all economy class layout, complete with large in-flight video screens for each passenger.

These slimly profiled economy seats provide extra legroom in each seat row while reducing the weight of the aircraft, which reduces fuel burn.

Landing in the shimmering heat haze of a sunny Chicago day on the A380's first ever arrival at O'Hare airport.

[above] The arrival press conference involved VIPs, Lufthansa management, and City of Chicago dignitaries who celebrated the first arrival of the A380.

[upper right] The inbound flight crew gives its full attention during the press briefing. The captain of the New York to Chicago flight is seen on the far right.

[right] The rubber smoke cloud billows behind the A380 after it touches down with 550 lucky passengers onboard.

A380 (F-WWJB) taxis in front of some massive Hong Kong high-rise buildings.

[above] A busy ramp scene as MSN 007 is serviced just minutes after arriving at the gates of Chek Lap Kok Airport.

[right] Large swarms of media were present to document this first A380 passenger-carrying flight to Hong Kong.

The passengers and crew of this China Eastern Airlines Airbus A300 admire the SuperJumbo on their way by.

A Qantas 767 lands beyond the tall tail of F-WWJB. Qantas will operate one of the largest fleets of the A380 when all ordered aircraft are delivered.

Four new orange chalks in place around the nose gear wheels ensure that the A380 is secured for servicing.

F-WWJB stands tall in front of the Airbus/Lufthansa route proving signs during the press conference.

A rare night shot with engine covers in place at Chek Lap Kok.

Signage at Chek Lap Kok Airport indicates the A380 will take off at 8:50. From Hong Kong the plane departed to Frankfurt before making its final flight to Washington, D.C.'s Dulles International Airport.

After its first flight into Washington, D.C., the A380 remains parked at the Lufthansa gate area after unloading its passengers.

MSN 007 departs on a brief VIP demo flight from Washington Dulles International Airport.

THE PEOPLE AND THE PASSION

People around the world, from the press to the aviation enthusiast, are fascinated by this giant airliner, including, of course, the passionate Airbus personnel themselves.

An Inuit couple, traveling by snowmobile, stopped to quench their curiosity about the giant airliner sitting in their backyard.

Nationalities the whole world over have always shown a great interest when the world's biggest airliner comes to town. These are the crowds witnessed in Guangzhou, China.

All eyes were on the A380 at Farnborough 2006!

A Chinese family in Beijing pays close attention to the servicing of the A380 at their hometown airport. Family airport trips like this were a common sight at every Airbus A380 destination.

A passionate Airbus crewmember proudly waves the Airbus flag after an aerial display flight at Berlin Air Show ILA 2006.

Contributors

AirUtopia Photographers: Scott Owen (Canada), Ma Shek Ching (Hong Kong), Kornphaka Peerawattuek (Thailand), Saliya Herath (Sri Lanka), Le Hieu Nghia (Vietnam), David Maxwell (USA), Matt Loewy (Australia), Gary Shephard (South Africa), Henry Tenby (Canada), Andres Ramirez (Colombia), Christian Lachtaras (Germany), Addisfortune.com (Ethiopia)

Writers: Bruno Pinheiro (Portugal), Scott Owen (Canada), David Maxwell (USA)

Photo Selection: Scott Owen (Canada), Saliya Herath (Sri Lanka), David Maxwell (USA)

Music (Select DVDs): Composed by Bruno Misonne (Belgium)

Special Thanks to: Tamrat G. Giorgis & Hailu Wondimu of Independent News & Media Plc, Publishers of Addis Fortune (Ethiopia)

Aviation Data Corporation/AirUtopia DVDs

For more information about Aviation Data Corporation and their extensive line of AirUtopia DVDs, please visit them online at www.airutopia.com. To purchase online, go to www.airutopia.com/retail.htm or email them at marketing@airutopia.com. If you have any old aviation films—including 8mm, 16mm, and Hi-8—kindly contact them at marketing@airutopia.com. Aviation Data Corporation is located in McLean, Virginia, just minutes from Washington DC. Telephone: +1 (703) 879-1976.

A380 (MSN004) at London Heathrow Airport, May 18, 2006.

The American Airport
ISBN 978-0-7603-1242-1

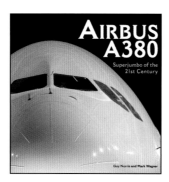

**Airbus A380:
Superjumbo of the 21st Century**
ISBN 978-0-7603-2218-5

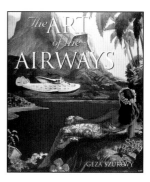

Art of the Airways
ISBN 978-0-7603-1395-4

A380 First Year

A380 Second Year

A380 US Tour

Dubai Airshow

Dubai Airport

Frankfurt Airport

Lumpur

Sydney Airport